ENSEMBLE DEVELOPMENT
Chorales and Warm-up Exercises for Tone, Technique and Rhythm
ADVANCED CONCERT BAND

Peter **BOONSHAFT** | Chris **BERNOTAS**

Thank you for making *Sound Innovations: Ensemble Development for Advanced Concert Band* a part of your concert band curriculum. With 399 exercises, including over 70 chorales by some of today's most renowned composers for concert band, it is our hope you will find this book to be a valuable resource in helping you grow in your understanding and abilities as an ensemble musician.

An assortment of exercises are grouped by key and presented in a variety of difficulty levels. Where possible, several exercises in the same category are provided to allow for variety while accomplishing the goals of that specific type of exercise. You will notice that many exercises and chorales are clearly marked with dynamics, articulations, style, and tempo for you to practice those aspects of performance. Other exercises are intentionally left for you or your teacher to determine how best to use them in reaching your performance goals.

Whether you are progressing through exercises to better your technical facility or to challenge your musicianship with beautiful chorales, we are confident you will be excited, motivated, and inspired by using *Sound Innovations: Ensemble Development for Advanced Concert Band.*

© 2014 Alfred Music
Sound Innovations™ is a trademark of Alfred Music
All Rights Reserved including Public Performance

ISBN-10: 1-4706-1823-0
ISBN-13: 978-1-4706-1823-0

Instrument photos courtesy of Yamaha Corporation of America Band & Orchestral Division

Concert B♭ Major (Your G Major)

1 **PASSING THE TONIC**

2 **PASSING THE TONIC**

3 **PASSING THE TONIC**

4 **LONG TONES**

5 **LONG TONES**

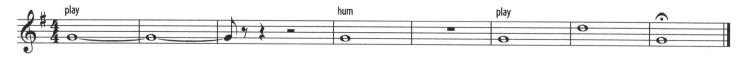

6 **LONG TONES**

7 **CONCERT B♭ MAJOR SCALE**

8 **SCALE PATTERN**

9 **SCALE PATTERN**

10 **CONCERT B♭ CHROMATIC SCALE**

11 **CHROMATIC SCALE PATTERN**

12 **FLEXIBILITY**

13 **FLEXIBILITY**

14 **FLEXIBILITY**

15 **CHROMATIC FLEXIBILITY**

16 **ARPEGGIOS**

17 **ARPEGGIOS**

18 **INTERVALS**

19 **INTERVALS**

20 **BALANCE AND INTONATION: PERFECT INTERVALS**

21 **BALANCE AND INTONATION: DIATONIC HARMONY**

22 **BALANCE AND INTONATION: LAYERED TUNING**

23 **BALANCE AND INTONATION: MOVING CHORD TONES**

24 **BALANCE AND INTONATION: SHIFTING CHORD QUALITIES**

25 **EXPANDING INTERVALS: DOWNWARD IN PARALLEL OCTAVES**

26 **EXPANDING INTERVALS: UPWARD IN PARALLEL FIFTHS**

27 **EXPANDING INTERVALS: DOWNWARD IN TRIADS**

28 **EXPANDING INTERVALS: UPWARD IN TRIADS**

29 **RHYTHM: SIMPLE METER (4/4)**

30 **RHYTHM: COMPOUND METER (6/8)**

31 **RHYTHMIC SUBDIVISION**

32 **CHANGING METER 6/8 AND 3/4**

33 **CHANGING METER 4/4 AND 5/8**

34 **CONCERT B♭ MAJOR SCALE AND CHORALE**

Chris M. Bernotas (ASCAP)

35 **CHORALE**

Randall D. Standridge (ASCAP)

36 **CHORALE**

Rossano Galante

37 **CHORALE**

Jack Stamp

38 **CHORALE**

David R. Gillingham

39 **CHORALE**

Andrew Boysen, Jr.

Concert G Minor (Your E Minor)

47 PASSING THE TONIC

48 LONG TONES

49 CONCERT G NATURAL MINOR SCALE

50 CONCERT G HARMONIC AND MELODIC MINOR SCALES

51 SCALE PATTERN

52 SCALE PATTERN

53 FLEXIBILITY

54 CHROMATIC FLEXIBILITY

55 ARPEGGIOS

56 ARPEGGIOS

57 INTERVALS

58 INTERVALS

59 BALANCE AND INTONATION: DIATONIC HARMONY

60 BALANCE AND INTONATION: MOVING CHORD TONES

61 BALANCE AND INTONATION: LAYERED TUNING

62 BALANCE AND INTONATION: FAMILY BALANCE

63 EXPANDING INTERVALS: DOWNWARD IN PARALLEL OCTAVES

64 EXPANDING INTERVALS: DOWNWARD IN TRIADS

65 EXPANDING INTERVALS: UPWARD IN TRIADS

66 RHYTHM: SIMPLE METER (4/4)

67 RHYTHM: COMPOUND METER (3/8)

68 RHYTHMIC SUBDIVISION

69 CHANGING METER 3/4 AND 6/8

70 CONCERT G MINOR SCALE AND CHORALE — Chris M. Bernotas (ASCAP)

71 CHORALE — Rossano Galante

72 CHORALE — Jack Stamp

73 CHORALE — David R. Gillingham

74 CHORALE — Stephen Melillo (ASCAP)

75 CHORALE — Andrew Boysen, Jr.

Concert E♭ Major (Your C Major)

76 **PASSING THE TONIC**

77 **PASSING THE TONIC**

78 **PASSING THE TONIC**

79 **LONG TONES**

80 **LONG TONES**

81 **LONG TONES**

82 **CONCERT E♭ MAJOR SCALE**

83 **SCALE PATTERN**

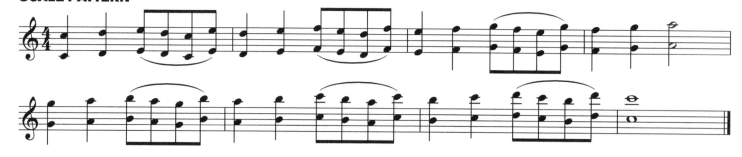

84 SCALE PATTERN

85 CONCERT E♭ CHROMATIC SCALE

86 CHROMATIC SCALE PATTERN

87 FLEXIBILITY

88 FLEXIBILITY

89 FLEXIBILITY

90 CHROMATIC FLEXIBILITY

91 ARPEGGIOS

92 ARPEGGIOS

93 INTERVALS

94 INTERVALS

95 BALANCE AND INTONATION: PERFECT INTERVALS

96 BALANCE AND INTONATION: DIATONIC HARMONY

97 BALANCE AND INTONATION: LAYERED TUNING

98 BALANCE AND INTONATION: MOVING CHORD TONES

99 BALANCE AND INTONATION: SHIFTING CHORD QUALITIES

100 **EXPANDING INTERVALS: DOWNWARD IN PARALLEL OCTAVES**

101 **EXPANDING INTERVALS: DOWNWARD IN PARALLEL FIFTHS**

102 **EXPANDING INTERVALS: DOWNWARD IN TRIADS**

103 **EXPANDING INTERVALS: UPWARD IN TRIADS**

104 **RHYTHM: SIMPLE METER (4/4)**

105 **RHYTHM: COMPOUND METER (12/8)**

106 **RHYTHMIC SUBDIVISION**

107 **CHANGING METER 4/4 AND 3/8**

108 **CHANGING METER 3/4 AND 5/8**

(3+2)

109 **CONCERT E♭ MAJOR SCALE AND CHORALE**

Chris M. Bernotas (ASCAP)

110 **CHORALE**

Ralph Ford (ASCAP)

Gentle

111 **CHORALE**

Roland Barrett (ASCAP)

Gracefully

112 **CHORALE**

Randall D. Standridge

113 **CHORALE**

Rossano Galante

Andante

114 **CHORALE**

Chris M. Bernotas (ASCAP)

Sweetly

10 **A tempo**

Concert C Minor (Your A Minor)

121 PASSING THE TONIC

122 LONG TONES

123 CONCERT C NATURAL MINOR SCALE

124 CONCERT C HARMONIC AND MELODIC MINOR SCALES

125 SCALE PATTERN

126 SCALE PATTERN

127 FLEXIBILITY

128 CHROMATIC FLEXIBILITY

129 ARPEGGIOS

130 ARPEGGIOS

131 INTERVALS

132 INTERVALS

133 BALANCE AND INTONATION: DIATONIC HARMONY

134 BALANCE AND INTONATION: MOVING CHORD TONES

135 BALANCE AND INTONATION: LAYERED TUNING

136 BALANCE AND INTONATION: FAMILY BALANCE

137 EXPANDING INTERVALS: DOWNWARD IN PARALLEL OCTAVES

138 EXPANDING INTERVALS: DOWNWARD IN TRIADS

139 EXPANDING INTERVALS: UPWARD IN TRIADS

140 RHYTHM ($\frac{5}{4}$)

141 RHYTHM: COMPOUND METER ($\frac{6}{8}$)

142 RHYTHMIC SUBDIVISION

143 CHANGING METER: $\frac{4}{4}$ AND $\frac{7}{8}$

144 CONCERT C MINOR SCALE AND CHORALE — Chris M. Bernotas (ASCAP)

145 CHORALE — Michael Story (ASCAP)
Andante

146 CHORALE — Rossano Galante
Lento, molto espressivo

147 CHORALE — Chris M. Bernotas (ASCAP)
Adagio

148 CHORALE — Randall D. Standridge

149 CHORALE — Stephen Melillo (ASCAP)
Rubato, slowly as felt

Concert F Major (Your D Major)

150 **PASSING THE TONIC**

151 **LONG TONES**

152 **CONCERT F MAJOR SCALE**

153 **CONCERT F CHROMATIC SCALE**

154 **SCALE PATTERN**

155 **SCALE PATTERN**

156 **FLEXIBILITY**

157 **CHROMATIC FLEXIBILITY**

158 ARPEGGIOS

159 ARPEGGIOS

160 INTERVALS

161 INTERVALS

162 BALANCE AND INTONATION: DIATONIC HARMONY

163 BALANCE AND INTONATION: MOVING CHORD TONES

164 BALANCE AND INTONATION: LAYERED TUNING

165 BALANCE AND INTONATION: FAMILY BALANCE

166 **EXPANDING INTERVALS: DOWNWARD IN PARALLEL OCTAVES**

167 **EXPANDING INTERVALS: DOWNWARD IN TRIADS**

168 **EXPANDING INTERVALS: UPWARD IN TRIADS**

169 **RHYTHM: SIMPLE METER (4/4)**

170 **RHYTHM: COMPOUND METER (9/8)**

171 **RHYTHMIC SUBDIVISION**

172 **CHANGING METER: 4/4 AND 7/8**

173 CONCERT F MAJOR SCALE AND CHORALE

Chris M. Bernotas (ASCAP)

174 CHORALE

Roland Barrett (ASCAP)

175 CHORALE

Rossano Galante

176 CHORALE

Chris M. Bernotas (ASCAP)

177 CHORALE

David R. Gillingham

178 CHORALE

Jack Stamp

Concert D Minor (Your B Minor)

179 **PASSING THE TONIC**

180 **LONG TONES**

181 **CONCERT D NATURAL MINOR SCALE**

182 **CONCERT D HARMONIC AND MELODIC MINOR SCALES**

183 **SCALE PATTERN**

184 **SCALE PATTERN**

185 **FLEXIBILITY**

186 **CHROMATIC FLEXIBILITY**

187 ARPEGGIOS

188 ARPEGGIOS

189 INTERVALS

190 INTERVALS

191 BALANCE AND INTONATION: DIATONIC HARMONY

192 BALANCE AND INTONATION: MOVING CHORD TONES

193 BALANCE AND INTONATION: LAYERED TUNING

194 BALANCE AND INTONATION: FAMILY BALANCE

195 EXPANDING INTERVALS: DOWNWARD IN PARALLEL OCTAVES

196 EXPANDING INTERVALS: DOWNWARD IN TRIADS

197 EXPANDING INTERVALS: UPWARD IN TRIADS

198 RHYTHM ($\frac{6}{4}$)

199 RHYTHM: COMPOUND METER ($\frac{6}{8}$)

200 RHYTHMIC SUBDIVISION

201 CHANGING METER: $\frac{4}{4}$ AND $\frac{7}{8}$

(2+3+2)

202 CONCERT D MINOR SCALE AND CHORALE

Chris M. Bernotas (ASCAP)

203 CHORALE

Robert Sheldon

Somber

204 CHORALE

Michael Story (ASCAP)

Andante

205 CHORALE

Chris M. Bernotas (ASCAP)

Andante

206 CHORALE: PRÄLUDIUM

Arcangelo Corelli (1653–1713)
Edited and Arranged by Todd Stalter

Adagio

207 CHORALE

Rossano Galante

Lento

Concert A♭ Major (Your F Major)

208 **PASSING THE TONIC**

209 **LONG TONES**

210 **CONCERT A♭ MAJOR SCALE**

211 **SCALE PATTERN**

212 **SCALE PATTERN**

213 **CONCERT A♭ CHROMATIC SCALE**

214 **FLEXIBILITY**

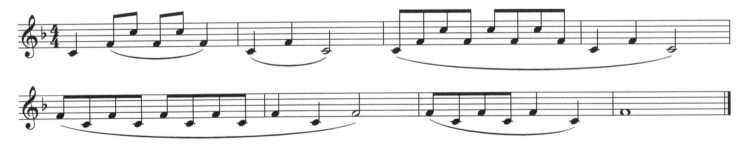

215 **CHROMATIC FLEXIBILITY**

216 **ARPEGGIOS**

217 **ARPEGGIOS**

218 **INTERVALS**

219 **INTERVALS**

220 **BALANCE AND INTONATION: DIATONIC HARMONY**

221 **BALANCE AND INTONATION: MOVING CHORD TONES**

222 **BALANCE AND INTONATION: LAYERED TUNING**

223 **BALANCE AND INTONATION: FAMILY BALANCE**

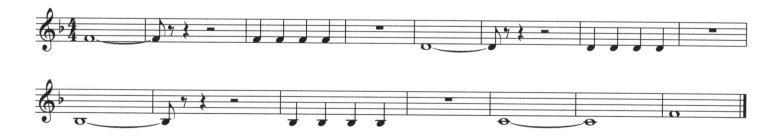

224 EXPANDING INTERVALS: DOWNWARD IN PARALLEL OCTAVES

225 EXPANDING INTERVALS: DOWNWARD IN TRIADS

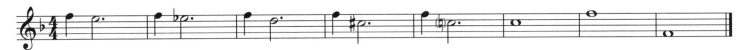

226 EXPANDING INTERVALS: UPWARD IN TRIADS

227 RHYTHM: SIMPLE METER (4/4)

228 RHYTHM: COMPOUND METER (9/8)

229 RHYTHMIC SUBDIVISION (4/4)

230 CHANGING METER: 4/4 AND 6/8 AND 3/4

231 CONCERT A♭ MAJOR SCALE AND CHORALE

Chris M. Bernotas (ASCAP)

232 CHORALE

Ralph Ford (ASCAP)

With reverence

233 CHORALE

Jack Stamp

Brisk waltz in 3

234 CHORALE

Chris M. Bernotas (ASCAP)

Moderately slow

235 CHORALE

Rossano Galante

Andante

236 CHORALE

David R. Gillingham

Flowing with grace and beauty

Concert F Minor (Your D Minor)

237 PASSING THE TONIC

238 LONG TONES

239 CONCERT F NATURAL MINOR SCALE

240 CONCERT F HARMONIC AND MELODIC MINOR SCALES

241 SCALE PATTERN

242 SCALE PATTERN

243 FLEXIBILITY

244 CHROMATIC FLEXIBILITY

245 ARPEGGIOS

246 ARPEGGIOS

247 INTERVALS

248 INTERVALS

249 BALANCE AND INTONATION: DIATONIC HARMONY

250 BALANCE AND INTONATION: MOVING CHORD TONES

251 BALANCE AND INTONATION: LAYERED TUNING

252 BALANCE AND INTONATION: FAMILY BALANCE

253 EXPANDING INTERVALS: DOWNWARD IN PARALLEL OCTAVES

254 EXPANDING INTERVALS: DOWNWARD IN TRIADS

255 EXPANDING INTERVALS: UPWARD IN TRIADS

256 RHYTHM: SIMPLE METER ($\frac{3}{4}$)

257 RHYTHM: COMPOUND METER ($\frac{12}{8}$)

258 RHYTHMIC SUBDIVISION

259 CHANGING METER: $\frac{4}{4}$ AND $\frac{5}{8}$

260 CONCERT F MINOR SCALE AND CHORALE

Chris M. Bernotas (ASCAP)

261 CHORALE

Chris M. Bernotas (ASCAP)

Menacingly

262 CHORALE

David R. Gillingham

Aggressive and forceful

263 CHORALE

Frédéric Chopin
Arranged by Michael Story (ASCAP)

Andante moderato

264 CHORALE

Jack Stamp

With purpose and resolve

265 CHORALE

Andrew Boysen, Jr.

Dark and dramatic

Concert D♭/C♯ Major (Your B♭ Major)

275   BALANCE AND INTONATION: MOVING CHORD TONES

276   BALANCE AND INTONATION: SHIFTING CHORD QUALITIES

277   EXPANDING INTERVALS: DOWNWARD IN PARALLEL OCTAVES

278   EXPANDING INTERVALS: UPWARD IN PARALLEL FIFTHS

279   CONCERT D♭ MAJOR SCALE AND CHORALE

Chris M. Bernotas (ASCAP)

280   CHORALE

Chris M. Bernotas (ASCAP)

281   CHORALE

Roland Barrett (ASCAP)

Concert B♭ Minor (Your G Minor)

282 PASSING THE TONIC

283 CONCERT B♭ NATURAL MINOR SCALE

284 CONCERT B♭ HARMONIC AND MELODIC MINOR SCALES

harmonic minor scale
melodic minor scale

285 SCALE PATTERN

286 SCALE PATTERN

287 FLEXIBILITY

288 ARPEGGIOS

289 INTERVALS

290 BALANCE AND INTONATION: LAYERED TUNING

291 BALANCE AND INTONATION: DIATONIC HARMONY

292 EXPANDING INTERVALS: DOWNWARD IN TRIADS

293 EXPANDING INTERVALS: UPWARD IN TRIADS

294 CONCERT B♭ MINOR SCALE AND CHORALE

Chris M. Bernotas (ASCAP)

295 CHORALE

Stephen Melillo (ASCAP)

Rubato, slowly as felt

296 CHORALE

Ralph Ford (ASCAP)

Passionato

Concert C Major (Your A Major)

297 PASSING THE TONIC

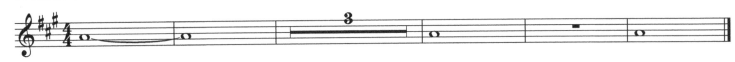

298 CONCERT C MAJOR SCALE

299 SCALE PATTERN

300 SCALE PATTERN

301 FLEXIBILITY

302 ARPEGGIOS

303 INTERVALS

304 BALANCE AND INTONATION: MOVING CHORD TONES

305 BALANCE AND INTONATION: LAYERED TUNING

306 EXPANDING INTERVALS: DOWNWARD IN PARALLEL OCTAVES

307 EXPANDING INTERVALS: UPWARD IN PARALLEL FIFTHS

308 CONCERT C MAJOR SCALE AND CHORALE

Chris M. Bernotas (ASCAP)

309 CHORALE

Chris M. Bernotas (ASCAP)

310 CHORALE

Robert Sheldon

Concert A Minor (Your F# Minor)

311 **PASSING THE TONIC**

312 **CONCERT A NATURAL MINOR SCALE**

313 **CONCERT A HARMONIC AND MELODIC MINOR SCALES**

314 **SCALE PATTERN**

315 **SCALE PATTERN**

316 **FLEXIBILITY**

317 **ARPEGGIOS**

318 **INTERVALS**

319 **BALANCE AND INTONATION: MOVING CHORD TONES**

320 **BALANCE AND INTONATION: DIATONIC HARMONY**

321 **EXPANDING INTERVALS: DOWNWARD IN PARALLEL OCTAVES**

322 **EXPANDING INTERVALS: DOWNWARD IN TRIADS**

323 **CONCERT A MINOR SCALE AND CHORALE**

Chris M. Bernotas (ASCAP)

324 **CHORALE**

Randall D. Standridge

325 **CHORALE: AIR, HWV 467**

Georg Fredrich Handel (1685–1759)
Edited and Arranged by Todd Stalter

Majestically
(opt. woodwind and bells 1st time, brass/percussion 2nd time)

Concert G Major (Your E Major)

326 **PASSING THE TONIC**

327 **CONCERT G MAJOR SCALE**

328 **SCALE PATTERN**

329 **SCALE PATTERN**

330 **FLEXIBILITY**

331 **ARPEGGIOS**

332 **INTERVALS**

333 BALANCE AND INTONATION: MOVING CHORD TONES

334 BALANCE AND INTONATION: SHIFTING CHORD QUALITIES

335 EXPANDING INTERVALS: DOWNWARD IN PARALLEL OCTAVES

336 EXPANDING INTERVALS: UPWARD IN PARALLEL FIFTHS

337 CONCERT G MAJOR SCALE AND CHORALE

Chris M. Bernotas (ASCAP)

338 CHORALE

Stephen Melillo (ASCAP)

339 CHORALE

Andrew Boysen, Jr.

Concert E Minor (Your C# Minor)

340 LONG TONES

341 CONCERT E NATURAL MINOR SCALE

342 CONCERT E HARMONIC AND MELODIC MINOR SCALES

harmonic minor scale   melodic minor scale

343 SCALE PATTERN

344 SCALE PATTERN

345 FLEXIBILITY

346 ARPEGGIOS

347 INTERVALS

348 BALANCE AND INTONATION: LAYERED TUNING

349 BALANCE AND INTONATION: DIATONIC HARMONY

350 EXPANDING INTERVALS: DOWNWARD IN PARALLEL FIFTHS

351 EXPANDING INTERVALS: DOWNWARD IN TRIADS

352 CONCERT E MINOR SCALE AND CHORALE

Chris M. Bernotas (ASCAP)

A

B

353 CHORALE

Michael Story (ASCAP)

Moderato

mp < *mf*

10

mp < *mf*

rit.

354 CHORALE

Chris M. Bernotas (ASCAP)

Mournfully

mf

< *f*

mf

9

f

Concert A Major (Your F# Major)

355 **CONCERT A MAJOR SCALE AND CHORDS**

356 **SCALE PATTERN**

357 **BALANCE AND INTONATION: MOVING CHORD TONES**

358 **CHORALE**

Chris M. Bernotas (ASCAP)

Concert F# Minor (Your D# Minor)

359 **CONCERT F# NATURAL MINOR SCALE AND CHORDS**

360 **CONCERT F# HARMONIC AND MELODIC MINOR SCALES**

harmonic minor scale   melodic minor scale

361 **SCALE PATTERN**

362 **BALANCE AND INTONATION: LAYERED TUNING**

363 **CHORALE**

Chris M. Bernotas (ASC

Concert D Major (Your B Major)

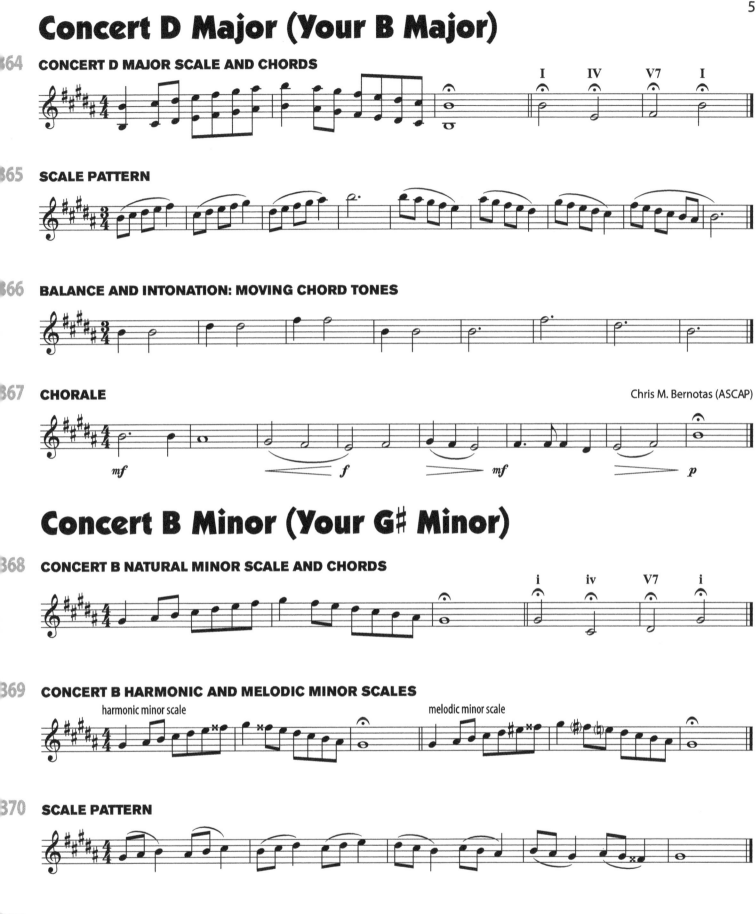

Concert B Minor (Your G♯ Minor)

Concert B/C♭ Major (Your A♭ Major)

373 **CONCERT B/C♭ MAJOR SCALE AND CHORDS**

374 **SCALE PATTERN**

375 **BALANCE AND INTONATION: PERFECT INTERVALS**

376 **CHORALE**

Chris M. Bernotas (ASCAP)

Concert G♯/A♭ Minor (Your F Minor)

377 **CONCERT G♯/A♭ NATURAL MINOR SCALE AND CHORDS**

378 **CONCERT G♯/A♭ HARMONIC AND MELODIC MINOR SCALES**

379 **SCALE PATTERN**

380 **BALANCE AND INTONATION: MOVING CHORD TONES**

381 **CHORALE**

Chris M. Bernotas (ASCAP)

Concert E Major (Your D♭ Major)

382 CONCERT E MAJOR SCALE AND CHORDS

383 SCALE PATTERN

384 BALANCE AND INTONATION: LAYERED TUNING

385 CHORALE

Chris M. Bernotas (ASCAP)

Concert C♯ Minor (Your B♭ Minor)

386 CONCERT C♯ NATURAL MINOR SCALE AND CHORDS

387 CONCERT C♯ HARMONIC AND MELODIC MINOR SCALES

388 SCALE PATTERN

389 BALANCE AND INTONATION: MOVING CHORD TONES

390 CHORALE

Chris M. Bernotas (ASCAP)

Concert F#/G♭ Major (Your E♭ Major)

391 CONCERT F#/G♭ MAJOR SCALE AND CHORDS

392 SCALE PATTERN

393 BALANCE AND INTONATION: PERFECT INTERVALS

394 CHORALE

Chris M. Bernotas (ASCAP)

Concert E♭ Minor (Your C Minor)

395 CONCERT E♭ NATURAL MINOR SCALE AND CHORDS

396 CONCERT E♭ HARMONIC AND MELODIC MINOR SCALES

harmonic minor scale   melodic minor scale

397 SCALE PATTERN

398 BALANCE AND INTONATION: LAYERED TUNING

399 CHORALE

Chris M. Bernotas (ASCAP)

Baritone Saxophone Fingering Chart

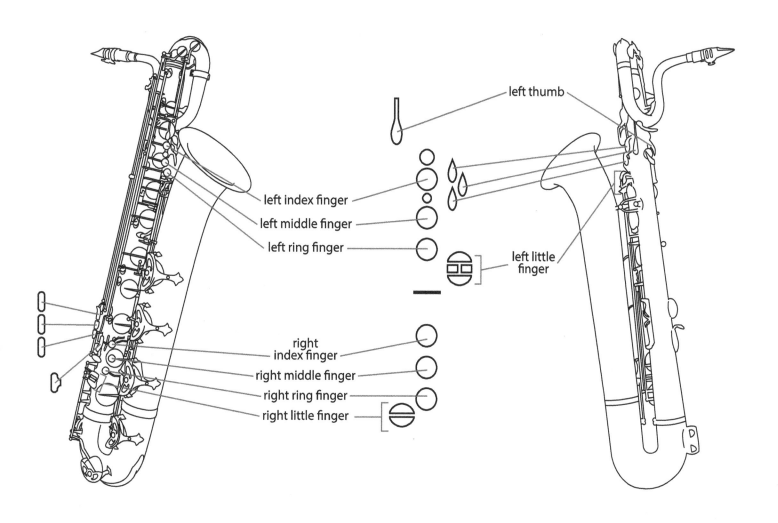

○ = open
● = pressed down

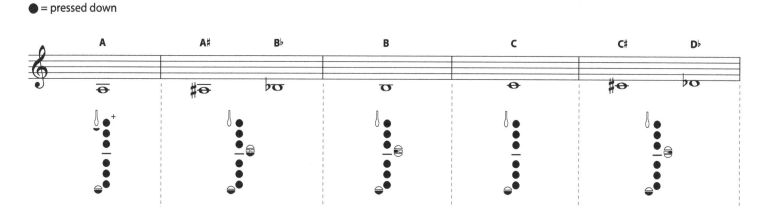

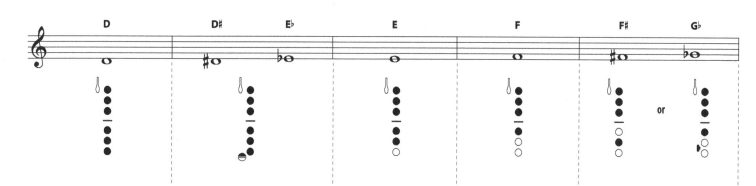

+This note is available on some baritone saxophone models.

56

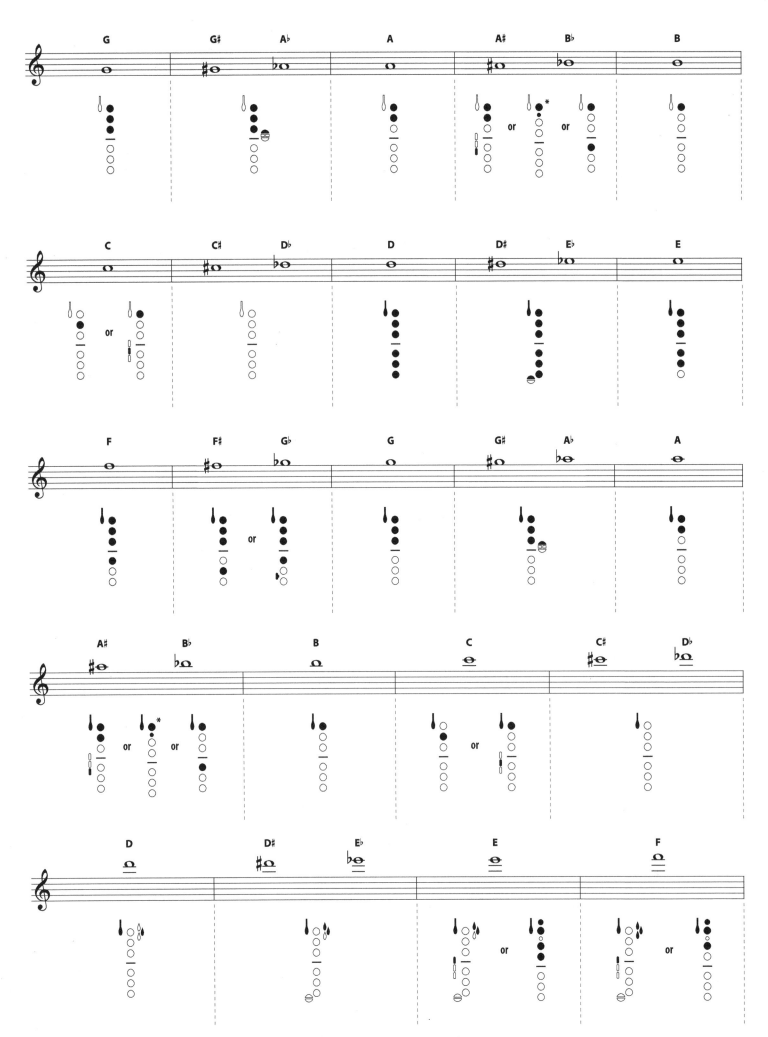

*The bis key is used for this fingering. This fingering should not be used in a chromatic scale.